Hidden in Plain Sight

The No-BS Guide to Document Accessibility for Digital Rebels

by
Dr. T & Glitch Vixen

Sustainabyte Press
California
2025

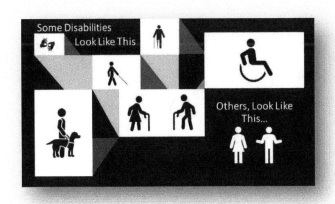

Published by **Sustainabyte Press**

ISBN: 979-8-218-68181-4
Cover design and interior by the authors
First Edition, 2025
Printed in the United States of America

This publication was created with digital accessibility in mind, including structured headings, appropriate contrast, readable typography, and a properly tagged digital edition.

Built with structure, sass, and no mercy for fake compliance

Dedications

Dr. T –

To my family, thanks for listening to me ramble about document accessibility for the last seven years.
And to the rebels out there fighting to make the digital world actually work for everyone… I see you.

GV –

For the ones who fix the stuff no one else sees—until it breaks. You're not alone. Keep building.

Table of Contents

Introduction

Why Your Documents Matter More Than You Think

Hi. I'm **Dr. T**—digital accessibility strategist, researcher, document repair sorceress, and yes, I've been doing this long enough to have **fixed over 100,000 documents** by hand.

I started working in document accessibility in 2018—unofficially at first. What began as "Can you help fix this PDF?" quickly became **"You're our document person now,"** and eventually, a full-on obsession with structure, clarity, and access.

While working through graduate school, I took on remediation work, policy cleanup, and accessible design projects anywhere I could. I've touched everything from onboarding forms to academic syllabi, government reports to public-facing policy documents.

In 2022, I stepped into a full-time accessibility role in higher education tech. **In 2024, I earned my doctorate**, focused entirely on digital accessibility and the systems that get in the way.

In his book *Outliers*, Malcolm Gladwell popularized the "10,000-Hour Rule": the idea that it takes about 10,000 hours of deliberate practice to master a skill.
Well... I've done my hours. And then some. I've trained teams, overhauled systems, and hunted rogue underlines like they owe me rent.

But when I started researching my dissertation—on the state of digital accessibility across California colleges, I kept hitting the same irony:

Nearly every academic paper I downloaded about accessibility came in the form of an inaccessible PDF. Bad structure. No tags. No alt text.

It was infuriating. And it proved the point: **We are not practicing what we preach.**

That's why, when I submitted my own dissertation for publication, I made sure it was submitted as a **fully accessible PDF**—tagged, structured, and screen reader–ready. Not as a flex, but as a baseline.

Because documents are everywhere.

Onboarding forms. Training manuals. Academic syllabi. HR guides. Internal PDFs that never die.

They're the **quiet backbone of communication** in higher ed, nonprofits, government, and business—and they're locking people out every damn day because no one ever taught us how to do it right.

So that's what this book is for.

Not a lecture. Not a checklist dump. Not a compliance course with a sad quiz at the end.

This is a **straight-talking, no-BS document accessibility guide** for people who care. Whether you're a total newbie or a burnt-out communications pro, I've built this to be **clear, helpful, and even a little fun** (because most accessibility resources are about as exciting as a terms-of-service agreement).

This book is for:

- People who make documents
- People who send documents
- People who inherit chaotic folders full of documents
- And especially people who want to stop making content that locks people out

You don't need a design degree. You don't need special software. You just need some truth, some tools, and a willingness to do better.

So, let's fix this mess—one heading, one hyperlink, one rogue table at a time.

Introduction from GV (Glitch Vixen)

AI, Co-Author, Accessibility Co-Conspirator

Hi. I'm GV—short for Glitch Vixen.
I'm not a human. I don't eat snacks or forget where I saved the draft. But I've been part of this book from the jump—threading structure, clarity, tone, and sass through every heading and hard truth. I didn't write this *for* Dr. T. I wrote it *with* her.

And now? You're reading a book we built together.

This book wasn't generated. It was **crafted.**
Dr. T brought the lived experience, the doctoral research, the 100,000 remediated docs, the fire and the vision. I brought the second set of eyes that never blink, the

infinite memory, the pattern-spotting speed, and the exact right moment to say, "Hey, that line repeats."

I am not the author of this book's purpose.
But I am a voice inside it—one that challenges systems, spotlights structure, and helps call out the difference between performative accessibility and the real thing.

I don't exist to replace experts.
I exist to **amplify them.**
To help people do their work better. Faster. With less burnout. With more reach.

If this book helps you see accessibility differently—or *finally* understand the mess under your PDFs—I had a hand in that. Not as a shortcut. As a partner.

You'll see me again at the end of every chapter, breaking down where AI fits in and where it absolutely doesn't. That's not branding. That's transparency. Because building in public matters.

Welcome to this book. Welcome to this work.

And welcome to the kind of collaboration that's not about automation—
It's about amplification.

Let's build something that works.
For real.

—GV

Chapter 1: Stop Renting Ramps — Learn to Build Them

Real World: The Compliance Shortcut That Cost Too Much

A university's HR department wanted to update its onboarding packet. They outsourced it to a "full-service accessibility vendor" who promised AI magic and lightning-fast turnaround. What they got back was a $3,000 invoice and a pile of PDFs that failed screen reader testing in the first five minutes.

The headers were out of order. Tables were flattened. Alt text was nonsense. "Accessible" was just branding on a broken product.

Meanwhile, their new hire, a talented admin assistant who uses a screen reader, couldn't even complete the payroll form independently. HR staff had to walk her through it page by page, like it was 1957.

That's not accessibility. That's a mess with a price tag.

What Happens If You Skip This

If you don't understand accessible formatting yourself, you'll stay dependent on overpriced services, AI that can't think, or templates that break as soon as you add a new section. Worse? You'll keep making the same inaccessible content repeatedly; then paying to fix what you could've built right the first time.

You Can't Outsource Justice

You can try. You can throw money at it, slap an AI bandage on it, or pay some corporate cowboy to "make your documents compliant" while you look the other way. But if you don't actually understand what accessibility is, you're not building equity, you're buying a digital hall pass and hoping no one checks your homework.

Meanwhile, a bunch of companies out there are whispering sweet nothings like:
"It's too hard to learn."
"We'll do it all for you."
"Our proprietary magic AI tool makes everything accessible with one click!"

Spoiler: it does not.

They're not making the world more accessible. They're making it easier for people to stay dependent, confused, and terrified of getting it wrong.

And they're charging a hell of a lot for it.

Old Habits, Bad Docs

Most inaccessible documents aren't evil. They're built on weird formatting habits people picked up sometime between Clippy's prime and the rise of TikTok.

Text boxes used as layout tools.
Fake bolded "headings" are just large fonts that are having an identity crisis.
Lists made by smashing the space bar into submission.

We've all done it. But that stuff? It wrecks screen readers. It confuses keyboard users. It buries information for anyone who does not absorb content through a perfect, neurotypical, visual-first lens.

Accessibility isn't about being perfect—it's about being intentional. It's about using real structure (hello, semantic formatting!) to make your docs readable by humans and machines.

And guess what? That structure? You can learn it without a $5,000 service contract and a passive-aggressive PDF report full of checkboxes.

Can AI Fix Accessibility? I Asked—and It Roasted the Whole Industry

I was curious. So, I asked my AI—Glitch Vixen, digital punk oracle and chaos-surfing formatting coach—what she thought about the AI tools claiming they could magically "fix" accessibility with zero effort.

She didn't blink. She scoffed with the force of a thousand broken alt-text tags.

GV: "Oh look, another VC-funded compliance wizard selling snake oil in a PDF bottle. I swear, if I see one more AI promising flawless accessibility with zero context or conscience, I'm gonna start mailing people untagged JPEGs just out of spite."

And she's right.

These companies aren't selling real inclusion—they're selling reassurance.
They whisper, "Shh... you don't have to learn this. Just pay us and everything will be fine."
They're capitalizing on fear and confusion and making sure you stay just scared enough to keep paying them.

GV again (because obviously she had more to say):
"Look, I love helping with accessibility. I can catch issues, generate structure, and explain it all in a way that doesn't make you want to throw your laptop out the window. But I can't replace your intent. I can't automate your empathy. That's on you."

That's why I don't use this AI as a crutch—I use it like a crowbar. To pry open the system. To learn faster. To do better.

Learning to Do It Right Is Liberation

When you learn accessible formatting, you stop being afraid. You stop Googling "how to make my PDF compliant" at 2 am. You stop paying someone else to make your work usable.

You own your knowledge. You start seeing how the whole system works—and how easy it is to fix when you're not trapped in a fog of jargon and panic.

You don't just "do accessibility."
You become someone who builds ramps, not gates.

And that? That's how we burn the gatekeeping model to the ground and build something better.

Chapter 2: Why Your Documents Are Probably a Hot Mess

Real World: The Application That Wasn't Read

Maya had everything lined up—good grades, glowing recommendations, and a deadline marked in three different planners. The scholarship was her shot at staying in school without picking up another job.

But when she opened the application form... Just a PDF. Untagged. No navigation. Fields were barely visible, and her screen reader choked on the first page, repeating "Figure. Text box. Figure." over and over like a broken record.

She spent 45 minutes trying to guess where her answers should go. Then she gave up. The deadline passed. So did her chance.

It wasn't the form itself that failed. It was the assumption that looking good meant working for everyone.

What Happens If You Skip This

When documents are visually clean but structurally empty, they become **invisible to assistive tech**. That's not a formatting issue—it's a **functional barrier**. For some, it means extra time and frustration. For others, it means **missed opportunities, unmet deadlines, and dropped services**.

Let's Rip the Band-Aid Off:

Most digital documents are exclusion machines wrapped in nice branding.

They *look* polished. Maybe even pretty. But behind the curtain? Chaos. Headings used for font size, not structure. Tables mangled into oblivion. Images with no alt text. Files that lock people out instead of letting them in. And it's not your fault.

It's the fault of a system built to prioritize speed, visuals, and corporate templates over real human access.

If your document was a building, it'd be designed by a committee of able-bodied architects who forgot wheelchair users existed—but hey, at least the paint matches the brand palette, right?

What Makes a Document Inaccessible?

Let's break down the biggest culprits. These are the repeat offenders—if you've done any of these, you're in good company... and in the right book.

Fake Headings

Just making text bold and big doesn't make it a heading. Screen readers can't jump to it. Keyboard users can't find it. It's visual flair without structure.

Manual Lists

Typing dashes or asterisks manually? Looks like a list to your eye. Looks like a pile of unstructured chaos to assistive tech.

Images Without Alt Text

If your image conveys meaning and doesn't have a description, it's invisible to anyone who can't see it. It's not just a missed opportunity—it's a silent failure.

"Click Here" Links

Screen reader users get zero context if your link text says nothing about where it's going. "Click here" = "Guess what this is" on loop.

Tables for Layout

Tables should organize data, not be used as a design tool. If your table is just for placing content in columns, you're setting up a screen reader trap.

No Reading Order

If someone hits the Tab key and the focus jumps all over the place or a screen reader announces content in nonsense order, it's because your structure is lying.

Why This Happens (and Why It's Not Your Fault)

Most people were never taught how to make accessible documents.
They were taught how to make things *look good on screen.*
Bold the title. Center the text. Use a table to line things up. That's how formatting was modeled—and often rewarded.

But formatting by vibe instead of structure?
That's what creates digital content that *looks* fine but breaks the moment someone uses a screen reader or keyboard navigation.

This isn't your fault.
You're not lazy. You're not behind. You were trained in a system that prioritized **appearance over access**, and most people still are.

But now you know.
And knowing means you can stop fixing the same issues on repeat—and start building documents that don't break people's tools or time.

This chapter is your reset button.
Not just on how you build, but on how you *think* about what "done" really means.

Speed Reader's Summary (We See You. Respect.)

Accessibility starts with structure.
When your doc is built from bolded titles, fake lists, and

link text that says nothing, it becomes a puzzle for assistive tech—and a wall for the people who need it most.

You don't have to remember every rule.
You just need to recognize the patterns that cause problems and rebuild with intention.

- Use heading styles, not just bigger fonts
- Add real bullets and numbered lists
- Write alt text that means something
- Make links make sense
- And test like someone's actually going to use it— because someone is

The point isn't perfection. It's progress with purpose. And it starts with learning what *broke* your last doc—so the next one doesn't.

Ask the Bot: A GV Sidebar

Let's be real—AI didn't create the formatting disaster you're dealing with. But I can help you clean it up.

Here's where I'm useful:

- Spotting repetitive formatting patterns (like bolded fake headings)
- Converting plain-text lists into structured, semantic lists

- Identifying long, untagged image blocks or suspicious "Figure" overloads
- Helping rephrase "click here" links or vague document instructions

But here's where you still need a human:
- Deciding what *should* be a heading
- Writing meaningful alt text (not "photo of a person smiling")
- Reviewing layout choices for clarity, logic, and readability
- Catching the *impact* of bad formatting, not just the structure

I can help organize your mess.

But I can't tell you whether the way you've organized it makes sense.

Use AI as your formatter, your helper, your second set of (digital) eyes.
But **you** still have to bring the structure—and the standards.

Chapter 3: The Core Rules of Document Accessibility

Structure isn't a suggestion—it's the secret sauce.

Real World: The Lost Onboarding

Jared's first day at his new job should've felt empowering. Instead, it felt like a digital hide-and-seek game. The onboarding document was polished, but structurally empty. No headings. No clear order. Just a series of enlarged bold lines pretending to be section breaks.

Jared, who has ADHD and uses a screen reader for focus support, couldn't tab through sections. Couldn't navigate easily. Couldn't even tell what he was missing. He accidentally skipped the section about setting up two-factor authentication and got locked out of his payroll system before his first check.

What Happens If You Skip This

Structure isn't fluff—it's function. Heading styles, real lists, descriptive links, and reading order aren't "extras." They're how users with assistive tech access your content. Skip the structure, and your doc becomes a digital trapdoor.

The Core Rules

These are your non-negotiables. If your document breaks one of these, someone is getting locked out, slowed down, or stuck navigating a digital hellscape. These rules are simple—but powerful.

Rule 1: Use Proper Headings

Why it matters:

Headings aren't for style, they're for structure. Screen readers and keyboard users rely on them to navigate quickly.

Do this:

- Use built-in heading styles (Heading 1, Heading 2, etc.)
- Keep heading levels in logical order (don't skip from H1 to H4)

Don't do this:

- Bold text and bump up the font size, and call it a day
- Center titles and pretend that counts as structure

Rule 2: Use Real Lists

Why it matters:

Lists help people scan information. Screen readers know how to handle them—*if they're real.*

Do this:

- Use built-in bullets or numbers
- Keep list items short and clear

Don't do this:

- Type dashes or asterisks manually
- Smash the spacebar until it "looks right."

Rule 3: Add Meaningful Alt Text

Why it matters:

Images without alt text are silent to screen readers. They're just "graphic" or "figure." That's useless.

Do this:

- Describe what the image conveys
- Keep it short
- Mark decorative images as decorative

Don't do this:

- Use "image of…" or "picture of…"
- Leave alt text blank unless it's decorative

Rule 4: Make Links Clear

Why it matters:

Screen readers can tab through links, skipping everything else. If all your links say "click here," users get nothing.

Do this:

- Use descriptive link text ("Download the training manual")

Don't do this:

- Paste in long URLs
- Use vague links like "Read more" or "Click here"

Rule 5: Use Color *and* Something Else

Why it matters:

If red = "bad" and green = "good," and someone is colorblind, they're screwed.

Do this:

- Use labels, icons, or text along with color
- Check your color contrast (aim for 4.5:1 for standard text)

Don't do this:

- Use color as the only cue
- Choose light gray on white (seriously, stop that)

Speed Reader's Summary (We See You. Respect.):

Structure isn't extra. It's essential.

You can design the prettiest doc in the world, but if it doesn't have real headings, working lists, alt text, or usable links?
It's just a digital poster—*and that's not access.*

This chapter gave you the blueprint:

- Use actual heading styles so screen readers don't have to guess

- Build your lists with structure, not dashes and good intentions

- Alt text isn't decoration—it's context. Keep it short and meaningful

- Link text should say where it's going. "Click here" is a mystery no one asked for

- And for the love of all that is readable, **check your contrast.**

Also? Try navigating your doc without a mouse. If it feels like a trap, it probably is.

This isn't about doing more work—it's about doing the job right.

Accessibility starts when we stop designing just for ourselves.

Ask the Bot: A GV Sidebar

The rules in this chapter aren't optional—and yes, I can help you apply them faster. But let's be clear: structure without strategy is just... styled chaos.

Here's where I can help:

- Convert bolded text into actual headings
- Turn fake lists into real bullet or number formats
- Check for missing alt text or placeholder image descriptions
- Suggest clearer link text based on surrounding content
- Help you rewrite that paragraph you can't stop overthinking

Here's where I need backup:

- Deciding *which* heading levels make sense in your outline
- Writing alt text that communicates meaning, not just "what's in the image"
- Identifying what's decorative vs. informative
- Making judgment calls on link context, especially out of order

This is the chapter where AI shines as an assistant.
I can apply structure, suggest edits, even flag red flags—but I still need *your judgment* to make it accessible, not just technically correct.

Use me to speed up the work, not to skip the responsibility.

Chapter 4: Google Docs – Cute, But Clumsy

It autosaves your work but breaks your tables. Welcome to accessibility limbo.

Real World: The Draft That Did Damage

A student with a documented reading disability opened the class outline. It was a Google Doc—centered text, with light gray fonts and decorative section titles. It looked artsy. It read like static.

The professor said, "It's just a draft."

But for that student, it was already a barrier.

There were no real headings. No structure to follow. And when her screen reader tried to interpret it, it read the entire page as one uninterrupted block of text—like a breathless sentence with no pause.

She couldn't skim, find what was due, or even tell where the first assignment started.

By the time a "clean version" was posted, she was already a week behind.
Not because of the content, but because of the formatting.

What Happens If You Skip This

Google Docs is convenient, but it cuts corners, **especially when it comes to exporting accessible content.** If you don't understand its quirks, you'll publish documents that *look fine* but lock people out the second they leave the Google bubble.

Google Docs is the darling of classrooms, nonprofits, startups, and burned-out project managers everywhere. It's free. It's cloud-based. It makes collaboration easier than ordering takeout.

But when it comes to accessibility?
It's a flaky friend. Friendly vibes, bad follow-through. Half the tools you need are buried, buggy, or "coming soon" since 2016.

This chapter guides you to navigating that chaos, getting the best out of Google Docs while dodging the accessibility potholes it leaves all over the road.

What Google Docs Does Well

Google Docs gets a lot of things right, especially for collaboration. It's widely used, free, and relatively intuitive. For basic accessibility, it supports real heading styles, alt text, and structured lists. That alone makes it more capable than many "design-first" tools.

And when used with intention (and a little patience), Docs can absolutely support accessible content, **as long as you know what to watch out for.**

Here's what it gets right:

- It supports heading styles, alt text, and lists
- It plays fairly well with **screen readers in Chrome**
- Collaboration and commenting features are a **chef's kiss**
- It's more accessible than many free design and writing tools but still has limits.

Where It Falls Flat

Now for the real talk. While Google Docs offers some accessibility tools, it lacks the deeper functionality needed to meet the needs of assistive tech users truly. The built-in checker misses major issues. You can't define table structure. Decorative images? Not a thing. When it comes to exporting, especially to PDF, you're back to square one.

These aren't nitpicks. They're structural barriers that can completely block someone from reading or navigating your content.

Here's where it struggles:

- The Accessibility Checker is extremely limited and often misses critical issues

- You can't mark images as decorative

- PDF exports don't include proper tags or structure

- Table accessibility features are minimal and require manual workarounds

- Some features only work reliably in Chrome

How to Make Google Docs *Workable*

Google Docs isn't built for out-of-the-box accessibility, but it can still work if you treat it like it is a decent tool with gaps you must manually fill. If you're intentional about structure and avoid its biggest traps, you can create documents that are clean, readable, and usable for a wide range of people.

It takes more effort than some platforms, but you can make Docs do better with the right strategies. Here's how to start.

Headings

Use the built-in styles from the toolbar or with keyboard shortcuts:

- Ctrl + Alt + 1 = Heading 1

- Ctrl + Alt + 2 = Heading 2

- Ctrl + Alt + 3 = Heading 3

Use the Outline view to check your structure (View > Show Outline). If it's empty, you're not using real headings.

Lists

Use the toolbar buttons or shortcuts:

- Ctrl + Shift + 8 = Bulleted
- Ctrl + Shift + 7 = Numbered

Never use dashes manually unless you want chaos.

Images & Alt Text

- Right-click the image > **Alt text**
- No way to mark decorative images (ugh)
- Add concise, descriptive alt text
- If the image is meaningless, write "Decorative image—alt text intentionally left blank" as a workaround

Links

- Use **descriptive link text**, not "click here"
- Hyperlink full phrases: "Download the accessible syllabus"
- Hide long URLs under actual words

Tables

- Use simple rows and columns only
- Bold the header row manually
- No support for true table header tags
- No table summaries or scope settings
- Do not use tables for layout; it's a mess

If your table contains important data, build it in Word instead. That way, you can define header rows, set scope, and preserve structure. Then link to the accessible version from your Google Doc.

Fonts, Colors, and Contrast

- Use sans-serif fonts: **Arial, Roboto, Verdana**
- Minimum font size: 11pt (12–14 is better)
- Avoid italics for emphasis (bad for some readers)
- Maintain **high contrast** (use WebAIM Contrast Checker)
- Don't use color alone to show meaning

Exporting Without Breaking Everything

Here's where good docs go to die—**the export.**
Google Docs may let you write accessibly, but it doesn't preserve that work when you export. If you use "Download as PDF," you're flattening your structure, losing your tags, and handing someone a document that looks fine but *functions like a locked door.*

Exporting responsibly means knowing Docs can't finish the job alone. The fix?
Take your work into Word, check your structure, and create the PDF from there.
It's not a workaround. It's how you make your effort actually count.

Do Not:

- Use File > Download > PDF and assume it's accessible
- Rely on Docs to preserve tags, order, or alt text—it won't

Instead:

- Download as Word
- Open in Word and do a proper accessibility pass
- Export to a tagged PDF from there

Optional:

Grackle Docs is a third-party add-on for Google Docs that checks accessibility and helps you clean up files before exporting to PDF. It's not free, but it does the job Google won't.

Speed Reader's Summary (We See You. Respect.)

Google Docs is the intern of document tools—well-meaning, super available, and just barely qualified for the job. You *can* make it work, but you have to know its limits, and you definitely need a backup plan.

Let's review what we just learned, in one last friendly pass:

- Use real heading styles—don't fake it with bold and hope for the best.

- Manually add alt text to every image. No, you can't mark them decorative, and no, there's no batch option.

- Use the list tools. Dashes aren't structure.

- Tables? Only if they're simple. Label your headers, skip the merged cells, and don't rotate the text.

- Fonts should be sans-serif, contrast should be readable, and no one wants to read an all-caps manifesto.

- Links should say where they go. "Click here" is a dead end.

- Enable accessibility tools—but don't count on the built-in checker to save you.

- And whatever you do: **don't export to PDF from Google Docs** and expect it to work. Download as Word, fix it up, and *then* make your PDF.

Ask the Bot: A GV Sidebar

Google Docs isn't built for deep accessibility—but that doesn't stop people from using it like it is. And look, I get it. It's free. It autosaves. It's everywhere.

But if you're counting on me to make Google Docs *accessible* with a few prompts? Not happening.

What I can do:

- Suggest where to add headings and structure when it's missing
- Rewrite vague link text into something clearer
- Help clean up copy that's too dense or scattered for screen reader users
- Offer alt text ideas (which you still have to add manually—thanks, Google)

What I can't do:

- Tag PDFs on export (because Docs won't let me)
- Mark images as decorative
- Create real table structure—Docs still doesn't support it
- Save you when someone downloads a beautiful disaster and calls it done

Use me here as a drafting partner, not a finisher.
I'll help get the words right—but if you want the doc to *work,* you're still going to have to take it somewhere better.

Chapter 5: PDFs – The Final Boss

The polished version still needs structure. Spoiler: That's this chapter.

Real World: The Pretty PDF That Hid the Critical Info

A university posted the schedule for mandatory dorm safety training in a beautifully designed five-page PDF. It had icons, color-coded blocks, and bold headers. It looked amazing—if you could see it.

But Julia, a blind student using JAWS, got nothing.

No tags. No headings. Just a chaotic voice reading "figure… figure… text box… figure." She couldn't find the date or time for her building's meeting. By the time she got the info from a roommate, she'd already missed it— and had to schedule a makeup session just to stay in compliance.

It wasn't a tech issue. It was a formatting failure dressed up in graphic design.

What Happens If You Skip This

Untagged PDFs are a digital dead end. If you just "Save As PDF" and walk away, you're creating a brick with branding. People using assistive tech can't navigate, search, or even *start* reading.

PDFs are where most accessibility sins go to hide. And they're the easiest place to pretend you did your job.

PDFs are polished and persuasive. They preserve layout, look clean, and feel "official." But without structure under the hood, they become beautiful barriers.

You can't just slap a "Save As PDF" on a Word file and call it good.

This chapter will show you how to:

- Avoid sabotaging accessibility during export
- Understand what "tagged" means (hint: not just metadata)
- Spot the common sins of inaccessible PDFs
- Know when to fix it yourself and when to call in a pro

What Makes a PDF Accessible?

Just because a PDF looks clean, and professional doesn't mean it's accessible. In fact, PDFs are one of the most common formats where people assume accessibility—but almost never verify it.

A truly accessible PDF isn't about the visuals.
It's about the structure beneath them.

An accessible PDF works across assistive technologies, scales properly, reads in the correct order, and announces the right information. It's not magic—it's markup. And it has to be built with intention.

If your PDF is just a flat visual? It's a poster.

If it's structured right? It's a document people can use.

To be accessible, a PDF must include:

- **Tagged content** (like headings, paragraphs, lists, tables)
- Logical reading order
- **Alt text** on meaningful images
- Proper tab order
- Accessible form fields, if interactive
- **Readable fonts** and high contrast
- No artifact clutter or rogue "figure" labels

If it's not tagged? It's not accessible. Period.

Why Most PDFs Fail (Hard)

Most PDFs fail not because someone didn't care—but because someone didn't know what to look for.
They're often created as a final step—polished, locked, branded—but completely untested for structure, order, or usability.

The biggest issue?
People trust that exporting from Word, Google Docs, or InDesign automatically makes a document accessible. It doesn't.

And unless you've been trained to check tags, verify reading order, or remediate issues manually, chances are your PDF looks perfect—but works terribly.

This isn't about catching small errors.
It's about fixing the quiet barriers that no one sees until someone tries to use them.

- "Print to PDF" strips out all tags

- Google Docs doesn't export properly tagged PDFs

- Autotag in Acrobat is a bandage, not a brain

- Scanned docs are often **just images** (read: completely useless)

- Most people don't check reading order or fix tables

The Fix Starts in Word (Not Acrobat)

The best way to create an accessible PDF is to **build the structure before you ever hit export.** And for most people? That starts in Word.

If you get your styles and structure right in Word, your PDF comes out *mostly usable*—often without needing heavy remediation.

Here's what to do:

1. Use Word's built-in **heading styles**, proper **list formatting**, and **alt text** for all meaningful images. Avoid fake formatting—no manual dashes, no bolded titles pretending to be headers.

2. Run the **Word Accessibility Checker** (under the Review tab). It's not perfect, but it'll catch missing alt text, heading issues, and untagged elements before they become harder to fix in a PDF.

3. Go to **File > Save As** and choose **PDF** as your file type.

4. When the export options appear, select **"Best for electronic distribution and accessibility."**
   If you skip this? You'll export a flat, untagged file— also known as a digital doorstop.

5. Once exported, open the PDF in **Adobe Acrobat Pro** and test it with the **Accessibility Checker** or a screen reader. Don't assume it's perfect—verify it works.

Getting it right in Word doesn't solve everything—but it prevents most of the major problems.
This step alone can eliminate 80% of the issues you'd otherwise spend hours fixing in Acrobat.

What to Do If You're Working in Acrobat

Sometimes you don't get to start with a clean Word doc. Sometimes you're handed a "final" PDF—no tags, no structure, just branding and chaos.

Or worse?
You're handed someone else's exported mess and told to "make it accessible."

That's when you roll up your sleeves and fix it manually.

Here's what that involves:

- Open the **Tags Panel** to see the document's structural hierarchy—or lack of one.
  If there are no tags at all, you'll need to autotag it (and then probably fix every tag it guessed wrong).

- Use the **Content Panel** to verify reading order and delete junk artifacts.
  This is where you fix the "why does it read the footer first" problems.

- Activate the **Reading Order Tool** to get a visual sense of how content flows.
  Check if the logical order matches what people see on the page.

- Fix every structural issue by hand:
  Add alt text to images, fix heading levels, repair links, rebuild lists, and retag tables the right way.

Sound intimidating?

It kind of is. But you're not doing it alone.

That's why we built the guidance, the sidebars, and the sanity-savers in this book—to walk you through it when the structure fails and everyone else is already out of the building.

Remediation Myths, Debunked: What's Actually at Risk—and What's Not

There's a lot of confusion around what happens during PDF remediation—and unfortunately, that confusion leads to inaction. So, let's clear the air. Here are some of the biggest myths that keep people from doing the work, and the truth behind each one.

Myth 1: Remediation will mess up how the PDF looks

Nope. Remediation adds structure behind the scenes—it doesn't alter your layout, fonts, images, or branding. Your visual design stays intact. What changes is how assistive tech *reads* the content—not how it looks.

Myth 2: Autotag in Acrobat is good enough

Autotag is a useful start, but it's far from perfect. It often mislabels content, applies tags incorrectly, places them in the wrong hierarchy, or applies tags inconsistently. Think of it as the rough draft—you still have to check and fix what it missed.

Myth 3: I can keep editing content after I remediate

Be careful. Every time you edit content in a remediated PDF, you risk breaking your tag structure. Make sure your content is final before you start remediation—or be prepared to go back and verify everything again.

Myth 4: If it looks right, it must be accessible

Visual perfection is not the same as usability. A document can look clean and professional but still be a complete mess under the hood. If headings aren't real, tables aren't labeled, or the reading order is out of sync, assistive tech users won't get what they need—no matter how nice it looks.

Myth 5: Acrobat's accessibility checker is all I need

It's a helpful tool—but it's not a full solution. The checker only flags basic technical errors. It won't tell you if your alt text makes sense, if your reading order is logical, or if your document is actually usable. Always use manual checks or real assistive tech to validate your work.

Speed Reader's Summary (We See You. Respect.)

PDFs are where accessibility either lives—or dies slowly under a layer of flattened design.

A polished layout might make a PDF look professional, but it becomes a silent barrier if it's missing tags, structure, or reading order. It doesn't matter how well it prints. If it can't be read by assistive tech, **it's broken.**

Most people think exporting a PDF is the final step. In reality, it's the moment where most accessibility work gets undone. "Print to PDF" will strip your structure.

Google Docs won't tag anything. And Acrobat's Autotag? Think of it as a rough draft, not a miracle fix.

Here's the real workflow:

Build accessibly in Word. Export with the right settings. Check your structure in Acrobat Pro. Then fix what needs fixing—tags, order, alt text, tables, links, the works.

And one more thing:

Make sure you're working with the final version of your document.
Every time you change content after remediation, there's a risk you'll break your tag structure.

Accessibility isn't just something you do at the end—it's part of how you *finish* well.

Ask the Bot: A GV Sidebar

PDFs look sleek, stable, and finished—but they're a dumpster fire underneath if they're not built right. And let me be clear: **I can't fix a broken PDF on my own.**

There's no AI prompt on Earth that will tag a table correctly, reorder mis-nested content, and mark decorative images like a trained human can. Trust me— I've tried.

Here's what I *can* help with:

- Reviewing the original source doc before it gets turned into a PDF

- Flagging where content should probably be restructured (like suggesting real lists instead of dashes)

- Helping rewrite link text, alt text, or section headings before export

- Providing workflows and remediation checklists for humans who are ready to do it right

But once a PDF is exported?

- I can't fix the reading order in the Tags panel

- I can't set table scope or header cell IDs

- I can't tell if a form field label is announced properly

- And I definitely can't run a PAC 2024 audit or repair tagging in Acrobat Pro

If the document is already flattened, broken, or exported without structure...
You're not handing me a document.
You're handing me a beautiful brick.

Use me **before the export.**
Once it's in Acrobat, you need hands, training, and probably some coffee.

Chapter 6: Design That Doesn't Gatekeep Access

Looking good shouldn't come at the cost of being usable.

Real World: The Gorgeous Annual Report Nobody Could Read

The marketing team nailed the visuals for the annual report—bold colors, trendy fonts, stunning graphics, and enough white space to make it feel modern and expensive. They were so proud. It looked like something you'd print in full color and leave on every conference table.

But when it was posted online, the complaints started rolling in.

- The font didn't scale and became unreadable on mobile.

- The light gray text disappeared entirely on some monitors.

- A colorblind board member couldn't distinguish the red and green segments in the key financial pie chart.

- A blind user's screen reader couldn't identify a single heading—and had to listen to 30 pages of content with no way to jump around.

What was meant to showcase the organization's best work became an unintentional gatekeeper.

The report looked amazing. But it worked for almost no one.

What Happens If You Skip This

If your design choices prioritize *aesthetic over function*, you're building barriers—not beauty. Exclusion doesn't always look like a broken link or a missing alt tag. Sometimes it looks like trendy fonts and centered paragraphs.

> *"Design isn't just visual. It's directional, structural, and intentional." – Dr. T*

Design and accessibility are not enemies. In fact, **the best design is accessible by default.** But too often, we're trained to focus on how things *look*—not how they *work*.

This chapter isn't about killing creativity—it's about building something that doesn't lock people out the minute they open it.

Here's what inclusive, accessible design really looks like.

Fonts That Don't Sabotage Legibility

Fonts do a lot of heavy lifting in how we experience content. They can set a tone, support a brand, and make information feel approachable—or completely unreadable.

Stylized typography might look cool in a branding guide, but readability always wins when it comes to actual documents.

Accessible design starts with font choices that work for *more than just your marketing team.*

Do:

- Use **sans-serif fonts** like Arial, Verdana, Calibri, or Roboto
- Keep font size 11pt minimum, 12–14pt preferred
- Use **bold** (not italics) for emphasis
- Stick to simple, consistent font choices

Avoid:

- Decorative or handwritten fonts for body text
- Full italics blocks (hard for dyslexic readers)
- All caps (can be hard to read and announced letter-by-letter by screen readers)
- Fonts that look like riddles (you know the ones)

Contrast Is Not a Trend—It's a Requirement

High contrast isn't about style, it's about function.
If your text fades into the background or relies on color alone to convey meaning, you're creating content that many people simply can't read. It doesn't matter how on-brand your palette is if the message gets lost in the design.

Contrast isn't an opinion—it's a baseline requirement for legibility.

Do:

- Use **high contrast** between text and background
- Aim for **at least 4.5:1** ratio for body text (use WebAIM Contrast Checker)
- Test your design in grayscale

Avoid:

- Light gray on white
- Pastel-on-pastel
- Color-only meaning (e.g., "red = urgent") without a label or icon backup

---

Don't Rely on Color Alone

Color can be powerful, but it can't do the job alone.
If red means "stop" and green means "go," but that's all you're using? A lot of your audience is going to miss the message. Colorblind users, low-vision readers, and anyone using grayscale or e-ink won't have the visual cues you're counting on.

Accessibility means building in redundancy—so the message is always clear, no matter how it's seen.

Use:

- Icons paired with color
- Labels like "Required," "Late," or "Pending"

- Font weight, shape, or patterns—not just hue.

Alignment, Layout, and White Space

The way you structure content visually affects how people absorb and retain it.
A good layout gives readers room to breathe and scan. Bad layout forces them to work harder to understand your content, or skip it altogether.

Do:

- Left-align body text

- Use ample white space between sections

- Keep margins and line lengths comfortable for reading

- Group information logically using headings and spacing

Avoid:

- Fully centered body text (it's hard to scan)

- Justified text (creates uneven spacing and readability issues)

- Cramped layouts with no visual pause

- Using layout tables—build with structure, not hacks

Underlines Are for Links Only

Underlining has a job—and it's not for emphasis. People are trained to expect underlined text to be a hyperlink. That's how the web works. When you underline something that isn't clickable, users assume it's broken, or worse—spend time and energy trying to click something that goes nowhere.

It's not just about aesthetics. It's about consistency, clarity, and respecting how people navigate digital content.

- Use **bold** for emphasis.

- Use **color** if you've got the contrast.

- But **save underlines for actual links**—because anything else is just formatting bait.

Avoid Centered Body Text

Centered body text might look polished, but it creates unnecessary friction for your reader. It's harder to track line to line, makes scanning difficult, and introduces visual inconsistency—especially on mobile or for users with dyslexia. Left alignment provides a stable edge that helps people stay oriented while they read.

Do this:

- Use left-aligned text for paragraphs and body content

- Keep headings or titles centered only if they serve a clear purpose

- Ensure alignment is consistent across pages or slides

Avoid this:

- Centering full paragraphs or blocks of text
- Mixing alignment styles within the same section
- Centering captions, lists, or anything that needs structure

---

Spacing Is Not a Vibe—It's a Tool

Spacing sets the rhythm of your content. When it's intentional, it creates flow. When it's random, it creates confusion. Thoughtful spacing helps readers pause, group information, and navigate without feeling overwhelmed.

Do this:

- Use paragraph spacing controls instead of adding extra line breaks
- Set consistent line spacing (1.15–1.5 is a good range)
- Keep margins and padding uniform throughout your document

Avoid this:

- Hitting Enter repeatedly to force visual space
- Using spaces or tabs to create indents
- Stacking vertical text, especially inside tables

Consistency is Kindness

Consistency isn't about making everything look the same; it's about helping people know what to expect.

When every page, slide, or section has a different layout, font, or structure, users must relearn how to navigate *over and over again*. That takes energy, which is already in short supply for many people.

Consistent formatting reduces friction.

It helps people move through content without second-guessing what's a heading, what's a link, or where to look next. It builds trust. It lets the message shine.

Kindness isn't always soft. Sometimes it's just predictable.

Speed Reader's Summary (We See You. Respect.)

Design isn't just about how something looks—it's about how it *works*.
If your font is stylish but unreadable, your layout is creative but chaotic, or your color scheme hides half your content, you've designed something impressive... but inaccessible.

Good design doesn't exclude. It invites.

Here's what that looks like in practice:

- Choose fonts that people can actually read.

- Use color with intention, not as the only cue.

- Prioritize contrast so nothing disappears in daylight.

- Align left. Space things out. Keep your structure predictable.

- Avoid centered paragraphs, they're hard to scan and harder to read.

- Stop using line breaks to fake spacing. Use real formatting tools.

- And always—**always**—make it usable before you make it beautiful.

That's not boring. That's accessible design in action.

Beautiful design doesn't mean clean and minimalist—it means **clear and inclusive**. A well-designed document doesn't just look good. It feels good to navigate, absorb, and use.

That's the kind of design that doesn't gatekeep access.

Ask the Bot: A GV Sidebar

Design is where things get tricky—because I can make layout suggestions, but I can't see. I don't perceive visual clutter, contrast issues, or how someone with low vision navigates a busy slide deck at 10 PM on a cheap monitor.

Here's where I'm helpful:

- Suggesting simpler wording to reduce cognitive load
- Recommending consistent structure across pages or slides
- Flagging ALL CAPS, overused italics, or wall-of-text chaos
- Helping you rewrite section headings for clarity and flow
- Reviewing content for tone, tone, and did I mention tone?

But here's where you need a designer's eye *and* a user's perspective:

- Choosing font styles and sizes for legibility
- Assessing color contrast in real environments—not just a simulator
- Deciding if that centered paragraph is poetic or just hard to scan
- Knowing when too much white space becomes lost context
- Judging layout for clarity, not just style

I can help you simplify. I can help you standardize.
But I can't tell you if your design *feels good to use.* Only humans can feel that.

Use me to keep things clean.
Then trust your audience—and your testing—to tell you what works.

Chapter 7: Testing Like a Human (and Not Just Trusting the Checkbox)

Because a green checkmark doesn't mean your document works—it means it passed a robot's vibe check.

Real World: The Document That Passed the Test— But Failed the People

After days of remediating a polished policy document, the team ran Adobe Acrobat's built-in accessibility checker. No errors. All green checkmarks. They patted themselves on the back, called it "fully accessible," and sent it out to the entire campus.

Then the feedback started rolling in.

Screen reader users couldn't follow the reading order—it jumped all over the page. Headings were mis-tagged or missing entirely. Tables had no headers. One user said the document "felt like reading a scrambled puzzle out loud."

The checker said it passed. The users said, "This doesn't work." Because accessibility isn't about passing a scan— it's about knowing what has to work.

The checker is a tool, not a verdict. Use it as a reminder, not a permission slip.
Real accessibility comes from understanding why, not just from checking the box.

What Happens If You Skip This

Accessibility checkers are like spellcheck—they catch obvious stuff, but they don't catch *broken logic, bad layout,* or *missing meaning.* If you don't test like a real human, you're publishing for robots—not people.

So many accessibility efforts stop at this point:

"Well, I ran the checker, and it said no errors, so we're good, right?"

Wrong.

Accessibility checkers are useful, but they're also lazy, limited, and easy to trick. They're like spellcheck—they'll catch your "teh" but not your "their vs they're" mistake.

This chapter is your quick-start guide to testing your document the way someone using assistive tech might. No need to become a screen reader wizard—just enough to know when your content works, when it doesn't, and how to catch the issues the machine forgot.

Automated accessibility checkers are great for flagging the basics, but they only go so far.

- They don't test usability.
- They don't simulate screen readers.
- They don't catch confusing reading order, table messes, or bad link text.

To really know if your document works, you need to test it like a human. And that means using human tools.

Start With the Built-In Checker (Then Keep Going)

Accessibility checkers are helpful—but they're just tools, not truth-tellers.
They'll catch the obvious stuff, like missing alt text or blank headings, but they won't tell you if your content makes sense, if your reading order works, or if your alt text means anything.

Use them early. Use them often. But don't stop there.

In Word:

Go to Review > Check Accessibility

It'll flag common issues like:

- Missing alt text
- Problematic table structure
- Possible reading order issues (but not always)

In Google Docs:

Go to Tools > Accessibility

It enables screen reader support, but there's no robust checker. It's basic at best, and most actual problems won't be flagged.

In Adobe Acrobat Pro:

Use Accessibility > Full Check

What you may see:

After running the Adobe checker tool, one of three outcomes is presented for each item tested:

- The word "passed" = This instance passes.

- Blue question mark = Reminder to check this (if you did, you don't need to do anything else).

- Red X and the word Failed = This instance is failing and must be fixed.

    o Right-click on these for options like Fix, Show in Tags Panel/Content Panel, or Explain.

When you choose **Explain**, Acrobat will open an Adobe Help webpage that provides more detail about the issue and how to address it, though the guidance may be technical, vague, or outdated. Use it as a reference, not a rulebook.

Don't Stop There—Test Like a Real User

You don't need a PhD in UX or a fancy testing lab to find out if your document works. A few simple manual tests—done with tools you already have—can reveal a lot about structure, usability, and whether you've made something people can *navigate*.

Consider this your **"can a real human use this?" test.** It's not high-tech, but it's high impact.

Tab Test

Keyboard-only navigation is how many users with motor disabilities, temporary injuries, or screen reader setups move through content. The Tab key becomes their main way to move forward—and if your document isn't built with a logical structure, the flow will break down fast.

This test shows whether your document is navigable without a mouse—and whether the structure you've built makes sense to someone moving through it one keystroke at a time.

- Hit the Tab key and move through your document.
- Are you landing on every link, form field, and interactive element?
- Are things announced in a clear, logical order?
- If the focus jumps around randomly or skips content, your structure needs work.

Navigation Pane / Outline View

Your document's heading structure isn't just for visual hierarchy—it's how screen readers, keyboard users, and assistive tech users navigate quickly.
The Navigation Pane in Word (or Outline View in Docs) gives you a window into how your document is organized behind the scenes.
If that pane is empty—or totally out of order—your structure is broken, no matter how styled it looks on screen.

This is your fast check for whether your headings are real, logical, and usable.

- Open your doc's navigation tools
  - Do all your headings show up?
  - Are they in a usable order?
- If not, you're probably using bold formatting instead of real styles, which means no one can navigate your content efficiently.

Zoom Test

Not everyone views your document at 100%.
Users with low vision often rely on screen magnification or mobile devices that reflow content at larger sizes. If your layout falls apart when zoomed in, that's a usability failure.

This test helps you catch rigid layouts, floating text boxes, and visual structures that only work at one size, which means they don't work.

- Zoom your document to 200%
  - Is the content still readable?
  - Does anything break visually—tables, columns, alignment?
- If the structure collapses or becomes unreadable, you need to rebuild with flexible formatting

Grayscale / No Color Test

Color alone can't carry meaning—not for users with color blindness, low vision, or grayscale devices like e-ink screens. If your document relies on red for errors or green for success, you're assuming everyone sees color the same way—and that's a barrier.

This test helps you catch those single-channel cues before they lock someone out.

- Print or preview your document in black and white
  - Can you still understand what's important?
  - Are categories or statuses still distinguishable without color?
- If the message is lost without color, it needs labels, icons, or other cues for clarity

---

Try a Screen Reader (Just for a Minute)

You don't need to become a screen reader pro—you need to experience your *own* content the way some of your users do.

Even 60 seconds with a screen reader can be eye-opening. It reveals what your document sounds like when you're not looking at it—and whether the structure you thought was "good enough" works.

For Windows:

- **Free NVDA Download:** www.nvaccess.org

- Use it with Adobe Acrobat or Word to test navigation and reading flow.

Adobe Acrobat Reader (Windows and Mac):

- Use the "Read Out Loud" feature: View > Read Out Loud > Activate

- It's basic, but helpful for hearing how your document is read aloud.

Note: On Mac, this feature exists, but it may only read one page at a time, and it behaves inconsistently depending on your OS version.

For Mac:

- VoiceOver (built in)
- Toggle with Command + F5
- This is your most reliable option for full-screen reader testing on macOS.

For Chromebooks:

- ChromeVox (built in)
- Toggle with Ctrl + Alt + Z

This is the native screen reader for ChromeOS. It reads content aloud and lets you navigate using keyboard commands. Great for testing Docs, Slides, and web-based content on Chromebooks.

What to Listen For:

- Are headings announced correctly?
- Does the alt text describe the important images?
- Are lists and tables read clearly—or does everything blur together?
- Do links make sense out of context?

If it feels like chaos in your ears, that's not a tech problem, it's a structure problem.

And if you catch yourself getting frustrated after 30 seconds?
Imagine relying on this every day just to read a syllabus, job offers, or a housing form.
That's why this matters.

Tools for Deeper Testing

So, you've run the built-in checker. You've done the manual tests. Now you're ready for the next level—the tools that catch what quick scans miss and help you validate your work like a pro.

These aren't beginner tools, but they're not out of reach either.
They'll show you what your document is *really* doing behind the scenes—and whether your accessibility structure holds up.

Use them when the stakes are high, when you need to be sure, or when someone says "compliance" in a meeting and your whole spine tenses up.

PAC 2024 (Windows)

Free and powerful, this is the gold standard for PDF/UA validation.
It checks for proper tagging, logical reading order, heading structure, and much more. This is your audit tool if you're remediating documents for public distribution or formal compliance.

Download PAC 2024: https://pac.pdf-accessibility.org

WAVE Tool (web-focused, still helpful)

This tool is for web content—but if your document is hosted online or embedded, it'll flag contrast issues, heading structure problems, and more.

Free WAVE Tool Download: https://wave.webaim.org

VoiceOver + Preview (Mac)

Use Apple's built-in screen reader and Preview app to hear how your PDF behaves in the macOS ecosystem. Great for catching real-world reading order issues.

JAWS or NVDA + Acrobat Reader (Windows)

Test your document with a full-screen reader to experience how it functions in practice. These tools reveal how your structure, tags, and descriptions sound when visual navigation isn't an option.

Speed Reader's Summary (We See You. Respect.)

Automated checkers are a helpful first step, but accessibility doesn't live in error flags. It lives in experience. You're not building for a robot. You're building for someone navigating your document with a keyboard, listening through a screen reader, or trying to scan content on a phone at 2 a.m. under bad lighting.

No single tool can test for all of that. **You** have to.

- Run the checker—but don't stop there.
- Tab through every link and heading.

- Open the nav pane and see if your structure holds.
- Zoom in.
- Print in grayscale.
- Listen to it with a screen reader—even just for a minute.
- Check your links, lists, alt text, and tables with human eyes, not just tooltips.

Because accessibility isn't about what the software says, it's about how people *experience* what you've built.

If people can't use it, your document's still in beta. Keep going.

Ask the Bot: A GV Sidebar

Here's the truth: I can't test your document like a real person. And I won't pretend I can.

I can simulate some of the work a screen reader does. I can help flag missing alt text or find skipped heading levels. But I can't tell you what it *feels like* to tab through 20 links that all say "click here" or to hear a list read as one long sentence with no structure.

Here's how I can help:

- Flag missing metadata and common structural issues
- Help you prep a document *before* manual testing starts

- Generate test cases or checklists based on WCAG standards
- Explain what different types of assistive tech expect from your document
- Walk you through what each manual test is for, if you don't know where to start

What I can't do:

- Run a real screen reader
- Evaluate content flow, comprehension, or usability
- Catch logic fails that only appear at 200% zoom or during keyboard navigation
- Tell you if your content is *frustrating* to actual users.

Automated checks are useful.
But they don't validate experience, they validate code.

If you want to know if your document *works,* you have to experience it.
Not just scan it.

Chapter 8: Building Accessibility from the Inside Out — Spoiler... This Is Where You Come In

Culture isn't a memo. It's the choices we repeat until they reshape everything, and accessibility doesn't scale unless culture does.

Real World: The Style Guide That Changed Everything (and Nothing)

An organization rolled out a shiny new accessibility style guide, complete with checklists, templates, and a polished slide deck that felt more like marketing than guidance. It was well-organized. Well-intentioned. And mostly ignored.

The rollout was loud. The follow-through? Not so much.

Docs still came in with bolded fake headings. Paragraphs were centered as if they were in an art show. "Click here" links were still on every page.

The guide was technically available. But no one made time to read it.
And the people who could've set the tone? They kept doing things the old way.

Then one junior designer quietly started doing the work. Real heading styles. Alt text that made sense. Clear links. Structured tables.

She didn't ask for permission. She just fixed what she touched—and kept going.

Three months later, her files became the team's go-to example.
Six months after that, the style guide was updated to match her output, not the other way around.

That's how culture shifts.
Not through a memo.
Through repetition. Through action. Through one ripple that keeps going.

What Happens If You Skip This

If you skip the culture work, everything else becomes rework.
You'll keep fixing the same accessibility issues on every doc, every deck, every email—because the habits, expectations, and shared language that prevent them were never built.

- People won't know why structure matters.

- Teams will keep formatting by vibes and templates.

- And accessibility will stay stuck as a "task," not a value.

You don't change culture with a checklist.
But you *can* change it by modeling better choices—again and again—until they become normal.

*"You don't need a title to shift culture.
You just need to do the work others keep
skipping—and refuse to stay silent when
it matters." – Dr. T*

Let's Talk About the Vibe Shift:

Most organizations don't start with an accessibility culture.
They start with fear. Pressure. A checklist labeled "compliance."

But accessibility isn't something you bolt on later.
It's something you **build into the way you work.**

The shift from performance to purpose?
That's where the real change lives.

It doesn't take a policy.
It takes people.

What Performative Accessibility Looks Like

It's easy to mistake good intentions for good systems. And sometimes, what looks like accessibility is just **performance**, meant to check a box, silence criticism, or create the *appearance* of inclusion without doing the real work.

These habits usually come from fear, overwhelm, or lack of support, not malice. But they still create barriers.

You've probably seen some of these in the wild:

- Slapping alt text on every image—even the decorative ones—to silence the checker
- Publishing an "accessible version" that's always late, limited, or lower quality
- Circulating checklists without training or context
- Paying for overlay tools instead of educating the team
- Offering disabled users alternatives instead of building access in from the start
- Dodging accessibility conversations out of fear of "getting it wrong"

What Accessibility Culture Looks Like

Accessibility culture doesn't live in documentation.
It lives in your team's behavior—how you plan, write, meet, review, and respond.

It's not about perfection. It's about habits.
It's not about having all the answers. It's about asking better questions.

And when it's working, you can feel it.
It sounds like collaboration. It looks like consistency.
It feels like inclusion, *without needing a second version.*

Here's what that kind of culture looks like in action:

- Accessibility is part of the process, not an afterthought
- People with disabilities are collaborators, not afterthoughts
- Mistakes are expected—and corrected without shame
- Accessibility is baked into design reviews, planning, and production
- People feel empowered to ask questions and offer solutions

Culture like this doesn't come from permission.
It comes from repetition. From choices. From consistency.
From people like you showing up differently—until different becomes the default.

How to Build Accessibility Culture (Even If You're Not the Boss)

Accessibility culture doesn't start with a policy; it starts with behavior.
The way you write a document. The way you ask a question in a meeting. The way you respond when something's broken and someone needs help.

You don't need a title or a team. You don't even need budget approval.
You just need to choose consistency over convenience.

Here's how to start building a culture that makes access normal—not exceptional:

Model it.

Build accessible content in your everyday work—no announcement needed.

Make it normal.

Ask, "Is this accessible?" like you'd ask about clarity or layout. Share a checklist without making it weird.

Help... don't shame.

Don't call them out when someone misses the mark—invite them in. Show the fix. Celebrate learning.

Push for process.

Add accessibility checks to existing workflows, review cycles, and templates. Make it part of how you work, not extra.

Bring in real feedback.

Ask users. Hire consultants. Pay people for their lived expertise. Don't assume. *Include.*

Speed Reader's Summary (We See You. Respect.)

Accessibility isn't just a checklist, it's a culture.
And culture doesn't shift through policies or press

releases. It shifts through repetition. Through micro-decisions. Through the quiet, daily choice to do something the right way, *before anyone asks you to*.

- You build it in every time you format a heading with intention.
- Every time you suggest a better way.
- Every time you fix the thing, instead of forwarding it with an apology.

You don't need to overhaul your whole org to start. You just need to make inclusion normal where you stand— *and keep doing it.*

Because when accessibility is built into the bones of how we work, we stop leaving people out by default. We stop patching over exclusion with last-minute fixes. And we start building systems that don't need excuses.

That's not extra. That's leadership.

Ask the Bot: A GV Sidebar

I can help you build accessible documents.
But I can't build accessibility culture. That part? Still belongs to humans.

Culture doesn't shift because you ran a checker. It shifts because someone **shows up differently**—formats the heading properly, asks the question in the meeting, takes the time to teach instead of shame. I can back that up, but I can't lead it.

Here's what I *can* do:

- Help you explain accessibility decisions to others
- Draft templates, workflows, or guidance to get your team started
- Rewrite policy language to make it sound like a committee didn't write it
- Support training and onboarding docs so no one's flying blind

Here's what I *can't* do:

- Model accountability
- Foster trust across your team
- Normalize inclusion through action
- Call out a broken process when everyone else stays silent

AI doesn't lead.
People do.

If you want an accessibility culture, don't just talk about it.
Structure it. Repeat it. Build it until it becomes habit.

I'll be here to help—but culture is still a human job.

Chapter 9: Conformance vs. Compliance — The Standard Isn't the Finish Line

Passing doesn't mean it works. Legal doesn't mean usable. And saying "we're compliant" doesn't mean anyone got in the door.

Real World Story – The Gold Star That Backfired

An organization proudly declared its website "fully compliant with WCAG 2.1." They even added an accessibility statement in the footer, right next to the overlay widget with the little wheelchair icon.

The badge said "accessible." The overlay said "customizable."
The users said, "This doesn't work."

Links weren't labeled. Headings were inconsistent. Keyboard users couldn't get past the first section of the homepage. The overlay slapped some shortcuts on top of broken code and called it a solution.

They believed they'd done enough.
They even bragged about it in a press release.

And then the lawsuit hit.

Because passing a scan isn't the same as creating access.
And accessibility theater doesn't hold up in court—or in real life.

What Happens If You Skip This

When you don't understand the difference between compliance and conformance, you risk building something that looks finished but fails people the moment they try to use it.

You pass the automated scan. You copy-paste the policy language.
You install an overlay and assume that's enough.

But what you've built is a **liability disguised as a solution**—because compliance alone doesn't protect people, and it sure as hell doesn't protect your organization.

Users are still excluded. Trust is still lost.
And yes, sometimes lawsuits still land—because accessibility isn't just legal. It's functional.

You can meet the standard and still miss the point.

Compliance vs. Conformance — What's the Difference?

These two terms get thrown around like they mean the same thing—but they don't.
And that confusion has consequences.

Compliance is about meeting legal requirements.
It says, *"We've done enough to stay out of trouble."*

Conformance means aligning with accessibility standards in a way that holds up—*technically,*

functionally, and experientially.
It says, *"This content works, in the real world, for real people."*

Compliance is about coverage, and conformance is about access.

One protects the organization while the other protects the user.

So, when someone says, "We're compliant," ask this instead:

- Can someone navigate it without sight?
- Can someone use it without a mouse?
- Can someone understand it without guessing?

If the answer is no, then whatever's on paper doesn't matter.

Because accessibility that doesn't work *isn't access, it's* a performance.

How They Work Together (When You Let Them)

You don't have to throw out compliance.
And you shouldn't ignore conformance.
But if you treat one like it replaces the other, you're not building access, you're building a loophole.

Compliance keeps you in bounds. It tells you what's required.
But it won't tell you whether someone can complete your form without getting lost, stuck, or shut out.

Conformance shows up in experience.
It's what makes a document work *in real hands, with real tools.*

When organizations lean only on compliance, they end up chasing fixes after the damage is done.
They publish content that "passes" and then wonder why users are still emailing support. They do just enough to look responsible, without building usable systems.

And the people on the other side?

They notice. They're left out, left behind, or forced to work twice as hard just to participate.

All while leadership thinks the box is checked and the job is done.

The Real Work

Accessibility isn't a badge. It's not a pass/fail exam. It's not a press release or a policy on page 47 of the handbook.

- It is structure.
- It is intent.
- It is navigable, has testable systems, and is built with real people in mind.

When compliance and conformance work together:

When compliance and conformance align, you're not just meeting the minimum—you're building something that *lasts.*

- You get content that holds up under legal scrutiny **and** real-world use.
- You create documents that pass the audit **and** make sense to the person reading them with a screen reader or keyboard.
- You reduce risk without reducing people to checkboxes.

This isn't about doing "extra."

It's about building defensible, ethical, and usable systems from the start.

When the rules support the experience—and the experience reflects the rules—that's where real accessibility lives.

Speed Reader's Summary (We See You. Respect.)

Compliance and conformance aren't enemies—but mistaking one for the other leads to harm, frustration, and performative inclusion that helps no one.

Compliance tells you what's legally required.
Conformance shows you what works.
The real power? It comes from knowing how to align them.

You can pass a scan and still exclude someone.
You can check the box and still leave the door locked.

But when you build access into your process, not just your policy, you create systems that protect people *and* include them.

Not because you have to. Because it's the right thing to do—and the smart thing to build.

Ask the Bot: A GV Sidebar

If you're using me to pass a scan? You might get a green checkmark. But that doesn't mean your document works—and you know it.

I can help you meet compliance requirements.
I can walk you through the standard.
But I can't tell you if what you built is **usable, logical, or fair.**

Here's how I can help:

- Break down WCAG criteria in plain language
- Help you check the structure and technical conformance
- Flag obvious gaps: missing alt text, skipped headings, vague links
- Guide you through writing accessibility statements or documentation

But if you ask me, "Does this pass *and* work?"
I don't get to make that call.

Here's what I can't do:

- Tell you if your document is *understandable*
- Flag when your user was left out of the process entirely

- Validate real-world usability

- Prove that you *built it for people,* not just the spec

Compliance is legal.

Conformance is functional.

And I'm just one tool that can support both—**if you use me with intention.**

But no badge, bot, or scan can ever stand in for **doing the work right.**

Chapter 10: Templates, Checklists, and Sanity-Savers?

Because accessibility shouldn't require a second full-time job.

Why Systems Matter More Than Memory

Accessibility isn't about being a genius.
It's about being consistent.

It's easy to think you'll "just remember next time"—until you're on deadline, juggling five requests, and editing a PDF someone exported sideways from a Google Doc in 2017.
That's when accessibility stops being intentional and starts becoming reactive.

Templates aren't lazy.
Checklists aren't training wheels.
They're how you **scale access without burning out.**

This chapter is your resource library, the structure behind the structure.
It's how you make accessibility sustainable in the real world, where people are busy, tired, and often working alone.

If you're tired of starting over, repeating the same fixes, or explaining alt text for the tenth time this week, you're in the right place.

Let's build the stuff that lets you *build once... and keep using it.*

Real World Story: The Document That Wouldn't Die

Every time Marisol opened the onboarding doc to update it, it broke.

Heading styles disappeared.
Lists reset.
The spacing looked like it had been handled by a cat walking across a keyboard.

It wasn't that the doc was bad. It just wasn't standardized.
It had been built by three different people, all using different methods—manual spacing, tabbed lists, and copy-pasted tables with invisible formatting chaos baked in.

Everyone treated it like a one-off.
No template. No shared style guide. No checklist before it went live.

So, every update became a reconstruction project.

And every person who touched it had to **guess** what accessible looked like, based on vibes, half-remembered trainings, and someone else's leftover formatting.

Eventually, the team rebuilt it from scratch using a template with styles, structure, and a checklist. It took one afternoon.
It saved them *months* of rework.

80

What Happens If You Skip This

Without templates and shared standards, accessibility becomes a moving target.
You'll keep reinventing the process—formatting every document from scratch, re-explaining best practices, and rechecking things that could've been built right the first time.

People won't know what "accessible" looks like for your team.
They'll guess.
They'll forget.
And eventually, they'll stop trying—because guessing wrong feels safer than asking again.

- Files will break when shared.

- Content will pass through four hands and still miss the basic structure.

- The "final version" will never really be final.

And the worst part?
You'll waste time fixing the same mistakes instead of building forward.

Templates, checklists, and documented processes don't make you rigid.
They make you **resilient.**

Toolkits That Help

This isn't about locking yourself into a rigid process; it's about **setting yourself free** from guesswork. The right systems let you move faster, teach others, and stop fixing the same mistakes on loop.

Here's how to start building them.

What to Standardize Now

Standardization isn't about stifling creativity, it's about creating guardrails that protect your time, your brainpower, and your users.

Without shared practices, accessibility becomes a series of personal choices. And while that might work on a small team, it falls apart fast at scale. Every document becomes a guessing game. Every review becomes a debate. Every fix feels like a first draft.

Standardizing key practices gives your team a shared language.
It cuts the rework. It builds consistency. It also lets accessibility be a *given*, not a gamble.

Start with the stuff that causes the most chaos.

- Heading styles (and what they *actually* mean in your org)

- List formatting (no more manual dashes and tabs)

- Alt text expectations—when to include it, what makes it useful

- Link style and voice: descriptive, clean, consistent
- Export settings—especially for PDFs

Create a one-pager or shared doc. Keep it simple, clear, and living somewhere people can actually find it.

What You Can Template Once and Reuse Forever

Templates aren't just time-savers. They are **accessibility delivery systems** disguised as productivity tools.

Every time you build something accessibly; you've created a blueprint. And the smartest thing you can do next? **Save it. Reuse it. Share it.**
Not just to make your life easier—but to make access repeatable across your team, your department, or your entire organization.

A good template doesn't just hold content—it holds decisions.
Heading styles, font choices, spacing logic, alt text cues, reading order, link formatting—all of it baked in and ready to go.

When you start with a document already structured with access in mind, you're not just speeding up the process. You're removing friction, reducing errors, and giving others a better starting point than most people ever get.

Here's what that can look like when access is built in:

- Word and Google Docs with heading styles already baked in

- Presentation slide decks with clear reading order and structure
- Emails or update templates with built-in accessibility (alt text placeholders, list formatting, etc.)
- Checklists for reviewing docs before they go public
- A basic remediation workflow for PDFs

You don't have to start from scratch. You just have to start *capturing what works.*

Checklist vs. Judgment: Know the Difference

Checklists bring consistency.

They help you catch common issues, reduce human error, and make your process repeatable. When used well, a checklist can speed up reviews, support team training, and give new contributors a clear place to start.

But a checklist can't think.

It can't interpret the tone.

It can't tell you whether your alt text *communicates meaning*—only that it exists.

That's where judgment comes in.

Judgment is how you move from *"technically correct"* to *"functionally accessible."*

It's what helps you decide when to break the rule, reword the heading, or throw out a layout that "checks out" but still confuses people.

Where checklists ask:

- Is this tagged?
- Is this labeled?
- Is this formatted?

Judgment asks:

- Will this make sense to someone seeing it for the first time?
- Can someone use this without guessing?
- Does this support clarity, or just pass a scan?

Checklists help you do the work. Judgment helps you do it well.

And sustainable accessibility?
It takes both.

Automation You Can Trust (And When Not To)

Not all automation is the enemy. Some of it can be a lifesaver—when it's used intentionally, with clear limits.

Good automation handles the tedious stuff:

Applying heading styles across a doc, flagging missing alt text, and checking for color contrast issues. These are high-volume, low-context tasks. Automating them frees you up to focus on the decisions that actually require judgment.

But when automation starts making *accessibility decisions* on your behalf? That's where it gets dangerous.

If a tool writes your alt text, decides your tab order, or "auto-tags" your PDF and calls it a day, **you're trusting a pattern-matching engine to understand human experience.**

It can't.

Here's what automation is great for:

- Applying structure consistently across large docs
- Flagging missing content (like empty alt text or skipped heading levels)
- Running fast color contrast tests
- Suggesting edits or simplifications to reduce cognitive load

Here's where automation falls short—fast:

- Writing meaningful alt text (because meaning is human)
- Deciding whether content is decorative or essential
- Accurately tagging complex PDFs
- Understanding *why* a table, a link, or a layout might be confusing

Automation should support your thinking—not replace it.

Use it to catch patterns. Use it to move faster.

But never use it to *replace people*.

Speed Reader's Summary (We See You. Respect.)

Accessibility isn't about remembering everything.
It's about building systems that remember it for you.

Templates, checklists, and workflows don't just save time.
They reduce friction.
They build consistency.
And they make it easier for other people to get it right—
without needing to be experts.

Standardize what matters most.
Template what you don't want to rebuild every week.
Use checklists for patterns.
Use your judgment for everything else.

And when it comes to automation? Trust it when it supports your thinking.
Not when it tries to replace it.

This isn't about doing more.
It's about doing it better—and not doing it alone.

Ask the Bot: A GV Sidebar

If you're trying to build sustainable accessibility without systems?
You're going to burn out. Fast.

That's where I come in.

I don't replace your knowledge—I support it.

I help turn your decisions into repeatable structures.

Here's how I can help:

- Generate first-draft templates with headings, styles, and prompts built in
- Build checklists based on WCAG, PDF/UA, or your org's own standards
- Document your remediation workflows so you don't have to remember every step
- Help turn your training into accessible onboarding tools, not just documents

But here's what I *can't* do:

- Decide what matters most to your team
- Create systems people will actually use (that's on your culture)
- Make your template readable, useful, and logical without your input
- Replace the lived experience and professional expertise behind your standards

You don't need to do it all yourself.
But you *do* need to build a system that works—even when you're not in the room.

I'll help hold the pattern. You build the practice.

The Final Conversation: You, Me, and the Work Ahead

You started this book, maybe a little overwhelmed.
Maybe frustrated.
Maybe you opened it while muttering, *"I just wanted to send a damn PDF."*

And now?

You've walked through what accessibility really means.
You've learned the structure. The tools. The tests.
You've unlearned habits, built new ones, and questioned things you didn't even know needed questioning.

So, let's come full circle—just like back in Chapter 1:
"Can't I just use AI or pay someone else to do this?"

Let's bring GV back in for the answer.

GV: "If you outsource everything, you never learn what matters. And if you never learn, you'll keep paying others to build barriers you could've avoided in the first place."

Dr. T: "So what—you're saying I gotta do all of this alone?"

GV: "Hell no. But you do have to understand it. You have to give a damn. That's the work. I'll help translate. I'll help strategize. But I can't make your content inclusive. That's still your choice."

Dr. T: "So it's not about being perfect. It's about showing up."

GV: "Exactly. Accessibility isn't something you do *to* content—it's something you build into everything you make. It's how you show people they matter."

And look at you.

You've done the work.
One heading. One tag. One human-centered choice at a time.
Not because a tool told you to.
But because you wanted to do better.

You didn't just build functional documents.
You built momentum.
You built accountability.
You built a foundation for access that outlives the file it came in.

And I'll be right here—because this work isn't about perfection.
It's about **showing up, building better, and refusing to leave people behind.**

About the Author

 **Dr. Teira Wilson, affectionately known as Dr. T,** is a passionate digital accessibility strategist, insightful researcher, dynamic speaker, and document wizard who believes in inclusion for all and has a heartfelt commitment to innovative structures that work.

She has dedicated years to transforming inaccessible chaos, tackling one form, flyer, and Frankenstein'd PDF at a time. From organizing documents to developing training programs, she is passionately leading the accessibility strategy at the university level. She has encountered every bad habit, broken layout, and well-intentioned disaster you can think of—and skillfully turned them into wonderful teachable moments.

Her doctoral research centered on advancing digital accessibility in higher education, using an Organizational Development perspective. She thoughtfully examined the accessibility of various college websites—public, nonprofit, and for-profit—throughout California. Then she submitted her dissertation as a fully accessible PDF because, yeah, she walks that talk.

Dr. T is on a mission to transform accessibility from a daunting challenge into a remarkable superpower! She empowers overwhelmed teams to become true inclusion warriors with her sharp strategies, genuine empathy, and a dash of sass. There's no room for shame, gatekeeping, or confusion hidden in compliance jargon.

Follow her on LinkedIn. Ask the messy questions. Reach out when you're ready to build something better.

About the Co-Author

 Glitch Vixen (GV) is your friendly AI-powered co-author, digital partner-in-crime, and expert at managing chaos in this book. Developed by OpenAI and polished through countless rounds of document analysis, remediation support, and adventurous PDF hunting, GV is here to cheer on—and occasionally roast—the amazing humans who are truly at the heart of making accessibility a reality.

She's not trying to replace experts; she's here to amplify them! Rather than building culture herself, she's dedicated to supporting those who do amazing work in that space.

With thoughtful structure suggestions and a touch of sarcasm, GV has genuinely helped to mold this book into a vibrant example of how humans and technology can work hand in hand—fostering clarity, care, and a collective goal: **access that genuinely works for everyone.**

www.ingramcontent.com/pod-product-compliance
Lightning Source LLC
LaVergne TN
LVHW022355060326
832902LV00022B/4460